DENNIS THE MENACE
SURPRISE PACKAGE

by Hank Ketcham

D0423501

FAWCETT GOLD MEDAL • NEW YORK

DENNIS THE MENACE—SURPRISE PACKAGE

Published by Fawcett Gold Medal Books, a unit of CBS Publications, the Consumer Publishing Division of CBS Inc., by special arrangement with The Hall Syndicate, Inc.

Copyright © 1968, 1969 by The Hall Syndicate, Inc.

Copyright © 1971 by Hank Ketcham

ISBN: 0-449-13860-7

Printed in the United States of America

20   19   18   17   16   15   14   13   12   11

"YOU'RE NEVER GONNA SCARE *NOBODY*, JOEY, IF YA DON'T LEARN TO SAY 'BOO' LIKE YA REALLY *MEAN* IT!"

"YOU BETTER *BURN* THIS! I THINK I JUST GAVE
MRS. TAYLOR A NERVOUS *BREAK-UP!*"

"ALL RIGHT! *ALL RIGHT!* IF YOU THINK HE'S IN BED, GO *LOOK!*"

"WHO'S NOT AFRAID TO GO DOWN TO THE 'FRIGERATOR WITH ME IN THE MIDDLE OF THE NIGHT?"

"...AN' ANOTHER NICE THING 'BOUT *FAT* BABY SITTERS:
THEY DON'T HARDLY EVER FOLLOW YA UP *STAIRS!*"

"WHY DON'T YA LET *MOM* PAY SOME O' THE BILLS? YOU ONLY GOT ONE PURSE, AN' SHE'S GOT *THIS MANY!*"

"...AN' THE GASOLINE COMES UP HERE AN' GOES.. UH ...WELL, COME ON! FIRST I'LL 'SPLAIN HOW A *TRICYCLE* WORKS!"

"MY DAD SAID *SOMEWHERE* THE SUN IS SHININ' RIGHT NOW! AN' *ANOTHER* GOOFY THING HE SAID....."

"GEE WHIZ! AN' YOU GUYS GET SORE WHEN I ASK FOR A GLASS O' *WATER!*"

"I'M MIXIN' UP MY MALT A LITTLE *BETTER!*"

"I DON'T THINK I SHOULD BE PUNISHED FOR PUTTIN' LIPSTICK ON MY NOSE! I WAS JUST TRYIN' TO MAKE JOEY *LAUGH!*"

"DAD, WOULD YOU PUT ON YOUR GLASSES AN' SEE IF RUFF
LOOKS *UNHAPPY* TO YOU?"

"BUT, DAD, I DON'T HAVE TIME TO USE THE OTHER BATHROOM!"

"HEY, MR. WILSON! YA WANNA BE A *HORSE*?"

"OH, DIDN'T I TELL YOU WHAT HAPPENED IN THE CELLAR?"

"WHICH WOULD YOU RATHER..."

"I NEVER SHOULDA ASKED."

11-16

"I CAN WAIT, PAL."

"THAT'S THE BOY! STEADY DOES IT....."

"BUT IF I WAS A CLEAN TYPE KID, YOU'D BE OUT OF A *JOB!*"

"YEAH, IT SURE *IS* A CUTE LITTLE DOG!"

"THAT'S THE LAST TIME I EVER LASSO AN *UNFRIENDLY* DOG!"

"WHY DIDN'T YA *TELL* ME THE HAMMER HEAD WOULD FLY OFF AND SMASH CAR LIGHTS?"

11-25

"I'M NOT NEITHER DUMB! *NOBODY* CAN FIX A BLACK-AND-WHITE SET SO YA GET COLOR!"

"HOW COME I NEVER GET WHISKERS? AN' I HAVEN'T SHAVED FOR *FIVE YEARS!*"

"DON'T WORRY, MRS. TAYLOR. I'M JUST FISHIN'.
I'M NOT *CATCHIN'* NOTHIN'!"

"I'M LOOKIN' AFTER YOUR STUFF. AN' I CHARGE THE KIDS A PENNY WHEN THEY BORROW A REAL *EXPENSIVE* TOOL!"

"WANNA DRAW STRAWS TO SEE WHO GETS THE OTHER *DRUMSTICK*?"

"DENNIS? OH, HE'S FINE. IN FACT, WITH ALL THIS NOISE
IT'S A WONDER HE ISN'T DOWN HERE!"

"I'M NOT SURE, JOEY, BUT I THINK YOU WEIGH HALF PAST FOUR."

"WHAT'S GOOD FOR GETTING A GOLF BALL
OUT OF A GAS TANK?"

"CAN YOU GIVE ME JUST ONE MORE CHANCE?"

"DENNIS CALLED WHILE YOU WERE OUT. HE WANTS YOU TO BRING HOME SOME *MORE* OF THAT *GOOD* PAPER!"

"I WAS PLAYING WITH DENNIS, AND THAT DUMB DOG OF HIS THOUGHT I WAS GOING TO *HURT* HIM!"

"WELL, IF I CAN'T PLAY WITH THAT, HOW 'BOUT PLAYIN' WITH SOME OF YOUR *OTHER* TOYS?"

"HOW DO I KNOW HE'S BEEN MESSING WITH MY CAMERA? BECAUSE THERE ARE SIX PICTURES OF RUFF AND TWO OF JOEY. *THAT'S* HOW 1 KNOW!"

"YEAH? WELL, YOU'RE GETTIN' TOO BIG FOR *YOUR* BRITCHES, TOO!"

"*SHE* CAN DISH IT OUT, BUT SHE CAN'T *TAKE* IT!"

"LET'S TELL MOM *YOU* DID IT. OKAY? SHE DON'T YELL AT *LITTLE* KIDS!"

"...AN' GOD BLESS MOST O' THE CATS AN' *ALL* THE DOGS!"

"...AND, AND I KNOW I SHOULDN'T HAVE, BUT I TOOK A NAP. AND, WELL, *HE HID MY TEETH!*"

"IF I'D KNOWN YA DIDN'T *LIKE* HORSE RADISH, JOEY, I'D HAVE MADE YOUR PEANUT BUTTER SAMWICH *PLAIN!*"

"WELL, YOUR SON IS READY. HE'S BLOWING THE HORN!"

"CHRISTMAS WILL SOON BE HERE! I JUST
SAW MY FIRST *SANTA CLAUS!*"

"...AN' HE'S GOT *TWIN BROTHERS* ALL OVER THE PLACE!"

"HEY, NOT SO *FAST!* WHERE'S *MY* PRESENT?"

"WHY DO ME 'N YOU GO THROUGH THIS EVERY DAY WHEN WE DON'T ENJOY IT?"

"SILENT NIGHT...HOLY NIGHT...ALL IS CALM...."

"YA WANNA KNOW SOMETHIN'? MOST OF THAT RED STUFF IN OUR THERMOMETER MUSTA *LEAKED OUT!*"

"ME AN' RUFF DON'T HAVE NO ELECTRIC BLANKET.
ALL WE GOT IS *EACH OTHER!*"

12-18

"HI! YOU PEOPLE STILL UP?"

"A **SUIT!** FOR CHRISTMAS?"

"MY DAD ALWAYS TRIES EVERYTHING OUT FIRST
TO MAKE SURE IT'S SAFE FOR ME."

"STAY ON THIS STREET UNTIL YOU COME TO A HOUSE WITHOUT A *FOR SALE* SIGN. THAT'S THE MITCHELL PLACE."

"WHICH DID YA LIKE BEST: THE COWBOY MOVIE, THE SERIAL, THE CARTOONS, OR SLIDIN' DOWN THE BANNISTER FROM THE BALCONY?"

"YOU'RE LUCKY YOU GOT A DUMB FRIEND LIKE ME TO PERTECK YA!"

"WILL YA DO ME A FAVOR, MR. WILSON? CALL MY FOLKS AND COMPLAIN ABOUT THE NOISE. THEY WON'T *LISTEN TO ME!*"

"WHAT'S SO GREAT ABOUT A KID LEARNIN' TO WALK? IF HE WAS LEARNIN' TO *FLY*, THAT'D BE *SOMETHIN'*!"

"I WISH YOU'D MAKE UP YOUR MIND. THIS MORNIN' YOU WISHED ME *HAPPY NEW YEAR*, AN' NOW YOU'RE SERVIN' *CARROTS!*"

"SURE, I TOOK IT OFF THE HOOK. I DIDN'T THINK YOU'D WANNA BE BOTHERED LISTENIN' TO A LOT OF *COMPLAINTS!*"

"IF YOU WANT CATSUP, *ASK* FOR CATSUP, AND NOT 'A SHOT OF RED EYE'!"

1-4

"WILL YA *TURN OFF* THAT VACUUM? I'M WATCHIN' *TELEBISHION!*"

"*FORGOT* TO SAY '*PLEASE*' AGAIN."

"WHEW! ISN'T THIS A LOT OF WORK JUST
TO FIND SOME SIDEWALK?"

"YA KNOW WHAT HE CALLED THAT NICE WHITE SNOW?"

"I DON'T KNOW *WHO* WON THE FIGHT. WE'RE GONNA FINISH IT AFTER LUNCH!"

"WELL, GEE, MR. WILSON ... IF SOMEBODY GOT *ME* OUT OF THE BATHTUB TO TALK ON THE PHONE, I'D BE *REAL HAPPY!*"

"BEFORE YOU GET MAD ABOUT OUR CLUB, MOM, WE DECIDED TO MAKE YOU AN *ORNERY MEMBER!*"

"NOW THAT MY FOLKS HAVE LEFT, I'LL
TELL YOU *MY* RULES !"

"*NO!* It's *NOT* OKAY IF YOU DUNK YOUR DOUGHNUT IN MY....."

"WELL, IF IT WON'T FLY, MAYBE IT'LL *FLOAT!*"

"THE SAFETY BELT ISN'T ENOUGH."

"I'LL HAVE A HOT DOG AND A *LONG FORK!*"

1-6

"WELL? IS THAT YOUR WORK?"

"HECK, NO! I DON'T KNOW NOTHIN' 'BOUT WASHIN' MACHINES! THAT'S *YOUR WORK!*"

"YA SEE, KID? IT'S A *TOUGH WORLD!*"

"C'MON JOEY! DON'T BE 'FRAID! THIS OL' PLUG CAN'T 'EVEN *TROT!*"

"I DON'T THINK WE LOOK GROWN-UP. I THINK WE LOOK *STUPID!*"

"MOM! COME HERE *QUICK!* MY YO-YO HIT
DAD'S PIPE AN' HE'S GONNA BLAME *ME!*"

"CAN I HAVE HIS CHOCOLATE AND HOT FUDGE
ICE CREAM DESSERT?"

"...HOTDOGS, CHILIBURGERS, 'TATOES N' GRAVY, TAMALE PIE...I CAN THINK O' *LOTSA* THINGS BETTER'N SCRAMBLED EGGS FOR BREAKFAST!"

"YOU SHOULDN'T TELL ME I'M BAD! I DON'T TELL YOU YOU'RE *UGLY!*"

"YOU DON'T LIKE ME BECAUSE I'M OF THE OPPOSITE SEX."

"AW, *BALONEY!* I DON'T LIKE YA 'CAUSE YOU'RE A *GIRL!*"

"...AND HIS MOTHER WAS WORRIED BECAUSE HE WANTED CATSUP ON HIS CARROTS. WELL, I TRIED IT AND, BY GEORGE, IT COMPLETELY *KILLS* THAT CARROTY TASTE!"

"WHY, IT'S NO TROUBLE AT ALL! I'LL JUST PUT ON ANOTHER PLATE."

"WHAT'S MOM SORE ABOUT?"

1-29

"WHAT A MESS! HE WAS EATING A PEANUT BUTTER AND JELLY SANDWICH, AND WHEN HE HEARD ME COMING, HE HID IT UNDER HIS *PILLOW!*"

"WE'RE MAKIN' A *JUNGLE* IN MY ROOM!"

"DON'T GET SO EXCITED, MRS. BELL! FROGS CAN *SWIM!*"

"MR. WILSON THINKS YOU GOT A *SWELL* VOICE! HE SAID YOU COULD WIN PRIZES CALLIN' HOGS!"

"BOY, I WISH I COULD SWIPE STUFF WITHOUT LOOKIN' NERVOUS!"

"LOOK, KID, I DON'T MIND YA DIPPIN' IN MY POPCORN, BUT WIPE YOUR HAND ON YOUR *OWN* PANTS, SEE?"

"DOES IT REALLY HURT? OR ARE YA JUST TRYIN' TO MAKE ME *FEEL* GOOD?

"MY MOM SENT YA SOME COOKIES, HERE'S MOST OF 'EM."

"I MADE SOME FUDGE. BUT I THINK I USED TOO MUCH MAYONNAISE."

"...BUT BEFORE IT BUSTED, MR. WILSON, WASN'T IT THE *BIGGEST* BUBBLE GUM BUBBLE YA EVER *SAW?*"

"CAN YOU WAIT A MINUTE? I HAVTA GO TO THE BATHROOM!"

"OKAY. I COUNTED ALL THE STARS.
WHAT SHOULD I DO NEXT?"

"WHILE WE'RE ALL IN A GOOD MOOD, MAYBE I OUGHT TO TELL YOU WHAT HAPPENED YESTERDAY."

"I *HAD* TO USE THEIR PAPER! I'M PAINTIN'
A *LONG, LONG* SNAKE!"

"... 'CAUSE MY MOM DON'T *LIKE* ME TO SLEEP IN MY CLOTHES!"

10-1

"THE KIDDIEGARTER TEACHER SENT YA
A NOTE. BUT RUFF ATE IT....."

10-3

"—AN' SHE MAKES HER *OWN* APPLE JUICE!"

"YOU WAIT HERE, DOCTOR. I'LL CATCH HIM!"

"IT WAS A WRONG NUMBER. AN'IF IT RINGS AGAIN, I'LL ANSWER IT."

"...AN' A PURPLE BATHTUB, AN' A PURPLE TOILET, AN' A PURPLE SOAP, AN' A PURPLE...COME ON! GO LOOK FOR YOURSELF!"

"YA KNOW WHAT 'WINDY' IS, DON'T YA? THAT'S *FAST AIR!*"

"WE BETTER WATCH OUR STEP THIS WEEK, SARAH. WE GOT A REAL CITY SLICKER STAYIN' WITH US!"

"THERE'S ONE THING YOU'LL ALWAYS FIND ON A FARM, DENNIS...PLENTY OF *FRESH VEGETABLES!*"

"YEAH, BUT I LIKE IT HERE *ANYWAY!*"

"HOW COME YA STAY AROUND THE FARM ALL DAY, UNCLE CHARLIE? DON'T YA EVER HAVE TO GO TO *WORK*?"

"IF I WAS HOME NOW, I'D STILL BE TRYIN' TO GET MY MOM AN' DAD OUT OF *BED!*"

"GEE, UNCLE CHARLIE, YOU GOT THE *BIGGEST* BACKYARD I *EVER* SAW!"

"IF YOU WANT TO *RIDE* OLD NELLIE I GUESS ITS ALL RIGHT. BUT SHE DON'T NEED NO *BUSTIN'!*"

"I DIDN'T MISS A *THING!* MR. WILSON SAYS THE NEIGHBORHOOD WAS *REAL QUIET* WHILE I WAS AWAY!"

"BECAUSE THERE'S BIRDS IN THAT TREE,
AN' THEY DON'T *LIKE* SMOKE!"

"I CAN'T COME OUT NOW.. I'M TAKIN' A *NAP!*"

"YOUR WINDOW'S NOT GONNA GET BETTER JUST 'CAUSE YOU KEEP THE FOOTBALL THAT WENT INTO YOUR LIVING ROOM!"

"WHILE YOU'RE BUYIN' YOUR SHOES,
I'LL BE IN HERE *SMELLING!*"

"I WAS GONNA RAISE YOUR SHADE AN' IT GOT AWAY FROM ME!"

"IF YA SEE A TALL, SKINNY MAN WITH GLASSES LOOKIN' FOR A SHORT KID, WILL YA TELL HIM I'M LOOKIN' FOR *HIM*?"

"I DON'T UNDERSTAND 'TWENNY DOLLARS AN OUNCE'. HOW MUCH CAN I BUY FOR TWENNY-FIVE CENTS?"

"WELL, IF THEY'RE PEARL'S, HOW COME *YOU'RE* WEARIN' 'EM?"

10-25

"OKAY, WHO TOOK MY PLATE WHILE
I WAS DANCING WITH BETTY?"

"MAYBE IT'S THE *LATE-LATE* SHOW FOR YOU. BUT IT'S THE *EARLY-EARLY SHOW* FOR ME!"

"I DON'T THINK YOU'RE GETTING ENOUGH *OATS!*"

"BOY! YOU SHOULD SEE WHAT YOUR OL' PEA SOUP
DID TO MY *WATER PISTOL!*"

"THERE'S NOBODY HERE BY THAT NAME. WHAT *NUMBER* DO YA WANT?"